# Arranging Your Financial and Legal Affairs

### A Step-by-Step Guide to Getting Your Affairs In Order

## Julie A. Calligaro

Women's Source Books Publishers
Grosse Ile, Michigan

ARRANGING YOUR FINANCIAL AND LEGAL AFFAIRS
A Step-by-Step Guide to Getting Your Affairs In Order

Julie A. Calligaro

Women's Source Books Publishers,
Post Office Box 99
Grosse Ile, Michigan 48138 U.S.A.

Library of Congress Catalog Card Number 97-062519

Printed in the United States of America
Book design Sans Serif
Cover design J. S. Graphics

International Standard Book Number 1-890117-07-2

Cataloging in Publication Data:

Calligaro, Julie A.
    Arranging your financial and legal affairs : a
    step-by-step guide to getting your affairs in order / Julie
    A. Calligaro.—1st ed.
        p. cm.
    Includes index.
    ISBN: 1-890117-07-2
    1. Finance, Personal. 2. Estate planning. I. Title.

HG179.C35  1998                                332.024
                                               QBI97-41617

*This book is dedicated with love to
Sheila Maureen Demery.*

# NOTE

---

I welcome your comments and questions, and I would appreciate hearing how this book helped you or how it could have been more helpful. Please write to Julie A. Calligaro at P.O. Box 99, Grosse Ile, MI 48138.

# CONTENTS

CONTENTS

# ACKNOWLEDGMENT

I gratefully acknowledge the invaluable contributions of Elizabeth P. Calligaro and Michael J. Morrin. Thank you.

# INTRODUCTION

## DO NOT PROCRASTINATE

Most people avoid putting their affairs in order until they are faced with a life-changing event, such as:

- Disease or illness which threatens death or disability;
- A family member or close friend dies unexpectedly;
- New responsibilities such as marriage or parenthood are assumed; or
- A lengthy trip is planned.

If your affairs are disorganized, don't wait until you face a crisis or an emergency. Take action now. Otherwise at your disability or death, your family, friends, or the local Probate Court will be forced to put your affairs in order.

Once you have completed this unpleasant but necessary task, you will feel in control of your life and you will experience a sense of relief and peace of mind.

## HOW TO USE THIS BOOK

This book guides you through the process of getting your affairs in order. Each chapter discusses a specific financial or legal topic. Read each chapter, even the ones that don't seem to apply. Otherwise you may overlook something that is relevant.

Most of the chapters include a Checklist which summarizes the actions recommended in the chapter. The Checklists are repeated on perforated pages at the end of the book. After reading a chapter, turn to the perforated section, tear out that chapter's Checklist and work through the list.

The suggestions in this book work for the young, the not so young, and those in between; for men and women; and for singles, married couples, and unmarried couples.

Turn to Chapter 1 and begin.

# 1

# ORGANIZATION

---

Your objectives are to:
1. Prepare an efficient record keeping system.
2. Locate and organize essential information.

## ESTABLISH A RECORD STORAGE AREA

Establish a permanent storage area for the records and documents that you will collect and organize. A fireproof legal size metal file cabinet with one or two drawers is a excellent choice. If that's not possible, purchase a 12" × 18" plastic storage box with cover. At the same, time purchase a box of legal size manila folders.

If you already have an effective filing system in place, purchase the materials that you will need to expand that filing system.

## RECORD KEEPING

Establish an efficient record keeping system. File your important papers in separate manila folders.

Label each folder and place the folders in alphabetical order in the file cabinet or storage box.

Decide if you will label the folders by general topic or by specific item and then be consistent. Keep in mind that in the event of disability and at your death, your spouse, children, or other loved ones will be working with your filing system, so aim for consistency and predictability as you label each folder.

To organize by topic, name the topic first, followed by the specific item contained in the folder. For example, "Investments-Mutual Funds-ABCFund," or "Mutual Funds-ABCFund."

To organize by specific item, name the item. For example, "ABCFund."

## INFORMATION TO LOCATE

Locate the information listed below that applies to you. Insert the information or documents in separate folders and label the folders.

1. Identification Numbers. On a sheet of paper, list social security number, military service number, driver's license number, and health insurance number for you and your spouse, if married; your children's social security numbers if they are minors, and any other identification numbers that you feel are important.
2. Tax returns.

3. Will, trust, trust amendments, power of attorney, medical power of attorney, and living will. **(Make copies of these documents. Return the originals to a safe place and store the copies in the folders.)**
4. Military discharge papers.
5. Insurance policies (life, disability, auto, homeowners, and health).
6. Birth certificates for all family members.
7. Marriage license.
8. **Up-to-date** information about each asset and debt. For example: bank statements, statements of brokerage accounts and mutual funds, stock certificates, savings bonds, statements of mortgage balances and other loan balances, statements of credit card balances, and titles to vehicles and boats.
9. Information about pension or retirement plans.
10. Closing or escrow papers you received when you purchased real estate.
11. "Buy-Sell Agreement" and all other documents related to the ownership of a business.
12. Divorce Judgment or decree if divorced.
13. Name, address, and phone number of physicians and other medical personnel that you currently consult.
14. Name, address, and phone number of accountant, attorney, financial planner, insurance agent, and any other advisors you currently consult.
15. Information about preplanned funeral arrangements, and burial information.

Store the folders in alphabetical order in the file cabinet or storage box.

## RECORDS STORED ON A COMPUTER

If some of your financial and legal records are stored on your computer:

1. Using the previous section as a guide, add any information that is missing.
2. Make backup copies of the records stored on your computer and put the copies in a safe place.
3. **Prepare a set of instructions for your spouse or loved ones so they will be able to access the information stored on your computer.**
4. Develop a filing system for the documents listed in the "Information to Locate" section which are not on your computer such as: will, trust, power of attorney, insurance policies, etc.

# CHECKLIST

## Establish A Record Storage Area:
## "Shopping List":

- ❏ a large box of legal size manila folders
- ❏ a legal size metal file cabinet, or
- ❏ 12" by 18" storage box with cover.

## Information To Locate
- ❏ Identification Numbers:

   * social security
   * military service
   * driver's license
   * health insurance number
   * children's social security numbers
   * other important numbers.

- ❏ Tax returns.

- ❏ Will, trust, trust amendments, power of attorney, medical power of attorney and living will. (**Make copies of these documents. Return the originals to a safe place and store the copies in the folders.**)

- ❏ Military discharge papers.

- ❑ Insurance policies.
- ❑ Birth certificates for all family members.
- ❑ Marriage license.
- ❑ Up-to-date information about each of your assets and debts.
- ❑ Pension or retirement plans.
- ❑ Real estate closing or escrow papers.
- ❑ "Buy-Sell Agreement" and other business ownership documents.
- ❑ Divorce Judgment or decree, if divorced.
- ❑ Name, address, and phone number of physician and other health personnel.
- ❑ Name, address, and phone number of accountant, attorney, financial planner, insurance agent, and other current advisors.
- ❑ Preplanned funeral, and burial information.

Store the folders in alphabetical order in the file cabinet or storage box.

### Records Stored On Computer
- ❑ **Make backup copies of computer records.**
- ❑ **Prepare a set of instructions so loved ones can access the information stored on your computer.**

# 2
# FINANCES

Your objectives are to:
1. Prepare an inventory of your assets and debts.
2. Determine if your assets are titled correctly.

## WHY PREPARE AN INVENTORY OF ASSETS AND DEBTS?

1. The inventory will help you determine if your assets are titled correctly.

2. The inventory will guide your spouse or loved ones through your financial affairs if you become disabled and at your death.

## HOW TO PREPARE AN INVENTORY OF ASSETS AND DEBTS

Turn to the perforated section at the end of the book and tear out the section titled "Inventory." Insert the date at the top. Consulting the information you accumulated about your assets and debts (Chapter 1), record the value of each asset and the amount of each debt.

To determine the market value of real estate, use the purchase price if the property was recently purchased or the appraised value if recently appraised. Otherwise, estimate the value by comparing your property to similar properties in the neighborhood that sold within the last six months.

The inventory used in this book contains a comprehensive list of assets and debts, so do not be surprised to see assets and debts included on the inventory that do not apply to you. Conversely, if you have an asset or debt that is not listed on the inventory, be sure to include it.

## HOW TO DETERMINE IF ASSETS ARE TITLED CORRECTLY

1. On the inventory, list the name or names which are on the title of the asset. The title will either be in one name, more than one name (joint ownership), or in the name of your trust.

2. Decide if each asset is titled in the correct name or names. For example, if you are married, is your name and your spouse's name on the title of each asset? If you are divorced, is your former spouse's name still on the title? If you have a trust, are your assets titled in the name of your trust?

Chapter 5 discusses the consequences of holding a title in one name, joint names, or in a trust.

3. Make a list of the assets which are incorrectly titled. If changes are necessary, take action immediately For example, if the title to your home is in your name alone and you want the title to be in both your name and your spouse's name, contact an attorney. If a bank account or savings bonds are incorrectly titled, make the corrections at the bank.

If your brokerage account is incorrectly titled, contact your broker. If you hold stock certificates that are incorrectly titled, contact the company and ask the name, address, and phone number of the transfer agent. Contact the transfer agent and ask what the procedure is for reissuing the stock certificates in the correct name or names.

## WHEN THE INVENTORY IS COMPLETE

1. When you have completed the inventory, label a folder "Inventory (Year)" and include the month and the year in which you completed the inventory. Make a photocopy of the inventory. Insert one copy in the folder. Attach the other copy to your trust. If you do not have a trust, attach the copy to your will.

2. Return the folders which contain the information about the assets and debts to the file cabinet or storage box.

## WHEN SHOULD THE INVENTORY BE UPDATED?

It is extremely important that your inventory always be up-to-date. Otherwise at your disability or death your spouse or loved ones may be unaware of assets that you have purchased or debts that you have incurred since the date of your last inventory.

Update the inventory every 12 months **AND** when you buy new assets, sell existing assets, pay off significant debts or incur significant debts.

When it is time to update the inventory, make a photocopy of the "Inventory" section located at the end of this chapter. Insert the date on the top line. Record the current value of each asset and the current balance of each debt.

Label another folder "Inventory (Year)". Make a photocopy of the inventory. Insert one copy in the folder. Attach the other copy to your trust or will, discarding the out-of-date copy. Repeat this process each time you update the inventory.

## HOW LONG SHOULD FINANCIAL RECORDS BE RETAINED?

Retain records which confirm:

- the date an asset was purchased,
- the purchase price of the asset,
- the date the asset was sold, and

- the selling price of the asset for four years after the date asset is sold.

Retain all other financial records, including tax returns, for three years.

To keep your record keeping system compact and efficient, put the folders which contain information about assets that have been sold in a separate section of the file cabinet or storage box. Label that section of the file cabinet "Assets Sold" and file the folders in alphabetical order.

## OPTIONAL: CALCULATING NET WORTH AND MONTHLY INCOME AND EXPENSES

If you are working through this book to arrange your affairs in preparation for disability or death, you may wish to include a record of your net worth and your monthly income and expenses.

## CALCULATING NET WORTH

Your net worth is the amount by which your assets exceed your debts. Once you have listed your assets and debts on the inventory, you will have all the information you need to determine your net worth.

To calculate your net worth turn to the "Net Worth" section at the end of the inventory. Insert the total value of assets where indicated. Insert the total amount of debt where indicated. Subtract the total

13

debt from the total assets. The difference is your net worth.

## MONTHLY INCOME AND EXPENSES

To determine your monthly income and expenses, turn to the perforated section at the end of the book and tear out the "Income and Expenses" section.

In the "Income" section, list the amounts of income you receive **MONTHLY**. If you receive income less often (or more often) than monthly, convert the income to its monthly equivalent and then enter it in the Income section.

For example, if you receive stock dividends of $300 every quarter, multiply $300 x 4 dividends. Your yearly dividend income is $1,200. Now divide the yearly dividend income of $1,200 by 12 months. Your "monthly" dividend income is $100. ($300 × 4 = $1200 ÷ 12 = $100 per month.)

Next, enter the amount of your monthly expenses in the "Expense" section. If you are billed for an expense less often (or more often) than monthly, convert the expense to its monthly equivalent and then enter it in the Expense section.

For example, if you pay a property tax of $3,000 twice a year, multiply $3,000 by 2 payments. Your yearly property tax expense is $6,000. Now divide the yearly tax expense of $6,000 by 12 months. Your "monthly" tax expense is $500. ($3,000 × 2 = $6,000 ÷ 12 = $500 per month.)

# CHECKLIST

## Inventory of Assets and Debts

❏ Record the value of each asset and each debt on the inventory located in the perforated section.

❏ Record the name or names on the title of the asset.

❏ Determine if each asset is correctly titled.

❏ If changes are necessary, take action immediately.

❏ Place the labeled folders in alphabetical order in the file cabinet or storage box.

❏ Label a folder "Inventory (Year)," make a photocopy of the inventory and insert one copy in this folder.

❏ Attach the other copy to your trust or will.

## Update the Inventory

❏ Update the Inventory yearly **AND** when you buy and sell assets, and incur or payoff large debts.

❏ Photocopy the inventory located at the end of Chapter 2 and insert the date.

❏ Record the value of each asset and each debt.

❏ Label another folder "Inventory (Year)."

❏ Make a copy of the updated inventory.

❏ Insert one copy in the folder and attach the other to your trust or will. Discard the out-of-date inventory.

# INVENTORY _____ (Date)

## ASSETS

| Type of Asset | Current Value of Asset | How Asset is Titled (Name, Names or Trust Name on title) | |
|---|---|---|---|
| **I.** **Cash Assets** | | **Value** | **Title** |
| 1. Cash on hand | | _____ | _____ |
| 2. Checking Account(s) (Bank and Credit Union) | | | |
| | | _____ | _____ |
| | | _____ | _____ |
| | | _____ | _____ |
| 3. Savings accounts (Bank and Credit Union) | | | |
| | | _____ | _____ |
| | | _____ | _____ |
| | | _____ | _____ |
| 4. Money Market account(s) | | _____ | _____ |
| | | _____ | _____ |
| **TOTAL CASH ASSETS** | | _____ | |

## II.  Investment Assets             Value        Title

1.   Certificate(s) of Deposit       _____     _____

2.   Treasury Bills                  _____     _____

3.   Stocks (List the company, number of shares and
     current price per share)

| Company | Shares | Price Per Share | Total | Title |
|---------|--------|-----------------|-------|-------|
| _____ | _____ | _____ | _____ | _____ |
| _____ | _____ | _____ | _____ | _____ |
| _____ | _____ | _____ | _____ | _____ |
| _____ | _____ | _____ | _____ | _____ |

Total Value of Stocks    _____

4. Mutual Funds (List the fund, number of shares and current price per share)

| Fund | Shares | Price Per Share | Total | Title |
|------|--------|-----------------|-------|-------|
| _____ | _____ | _____ | _____ | _____ |
| _____ | _____ | _____ | _____ | _____ |
| _____ | _____ | _____ | _____ | _____ |
| _____ | _____ | _____ | _____ | _____ |

Total Value of Mutual Funds  _____

5.   U.S. Savings Bonds  _____  _____

6.   Municipal Bonds  _____  _____

7.   Corporate Bonds  _____  _____

**TOTAL INVESTMENT ASSETS**  _____

| **III.** **Real Estate** | **Value** | **Title** |
|---------|-------|-------|
| 1.   Residence | _____ | _____ |
| 2.   Vacation Home | _____ | _____ |
| 3.   Vacant Land | _____ | _____ |
| **Total of Real Estate Assets** | _____ | |

## IV. Retirement/Pension/ Profit Sharing

| | Value | Title |
|---|---|---|
| 1. IRA Accounts | ___ | ___ |
| 2. Keogh Accounts | ___ | ___ |
| 3. Pension/Profit Sharing Plans, 401(k), Thrift Savings, Stock Purchase | ___ | ___ |

**Total of Retirement/Pension/ Profit Sharing** ___

## V. Miscellaneous

| | Value | Title |
|---|---|---|
| 1. Limited Partnerships | ___ | ___ |
| 2. Notes, Mortgages or Other Debts Owed To You | ___ | ___ |
| 3. Other | ___ | ___ |
| | ___ | ___ |
| | ___ | ___ |

**Total of Miscellaneous Assets** ___

**VI. Business Ownership** ___ ___

| VII. Vehicles\Boats | Value | Title |
|---|---|---|
| ___ | ___ | ___ |
| ___ | ___ | ___ |
| ___ | ___ | ___ |

## Totals of Assets:

I. Cash _____

II. Investment Assets _____

III. Real Estate Assets _____

IV. Retirement Assets _____

V. Miscellaneous Assets _____

VI. Business Ownership Assets _____

VII. Vehicles\Boats _____

**TOTAL VALUE OF ALL ASSETS** _____

## DEBTS (LIABILITIES)

**Type of Debt**                     **Current Balance**

1. Mortgage (Residence) _____

2. Mortgage (Vacation Home) _____

3. Home Equity Loan _____

4. Auto Loan _____

5. Auto Loan _____

6. Credit Card _____

7. Credit Card _____

8. Credit Card _____

9. Student Loan _____

9. Life Insurance Loan _____

10. Other Loan(s) _____

**Total Debt** _____

## NET WORTH:
## TOTAL VALUE OF ALL ASSETS       ———
## MINUS YOUR TOTAL DEBT       ———
## YOUR NET WORTH IS       ———

# INCOME AND EXPENSES

## INCOME

| Income | Amount Received Each Month |
|---|---|
| 1. Salary | _____ |
| 2. Social Security | _____ |
| 3. Pension-Retirement Benefits | _____ |
| 4. Annuity Payments | _____ |
| 5. Rental Income | _____ |
| 6. Interest | _____ |
| 7. Dividends | _____ |
| 8. Child Support | _____ |
| 9. Other | _____ |
| **Total Income** | _____ |

## EXPENSES

| Expense | Amount of Monthly Expense |
|---|---|
| I. Home | |
| 1. Mortgage or Rent | _____ |
| 2. Home Equity Loan Payment | _____ |
| 3. Property Taxes | _____ |
| 4. Insurance | _____ |
| 5. Association Dues | _____ |
| 6. Utilities | _____ |

a. Heating Fuel     _____
b. Gas     _____
c. Electric     _____
d. Water and Sewer     _____
e. Telephone     _____
f. Cable TV     _____
7. Repairs     _____

**Total Home Expenses**     _____

II. Living
1. Food     _____
2. Clothing     _____
3. Child Care     _____
4. Transportation
   a. Auto Loan Payment     _____
   b. Auto Lease Payment     _____
   c. Auto Insurance     _____
   d. Gas and Oil     _____
   e. Repairs     _____
   f. Commuting expenses     _____
5. Pet Care     _____
6. Entertainment     _____

**Total Living Expenses**     _____

III. Medical
1. Health Insurance Premiums     _____
2. Dental Insurance Premiums     _____
3. Medicare Payments     _____
4. Doctor Visits     _____
5. Dental Care     _____
6. Eyeglasses     _____

7. Prescriptions  _____
8. Medical Supplies  _____
8. Miscellaneous Medical Expenses  _____
    **Total Medical Expenses**  _____

IV.  Loans (other than mortgage and home equity loans) and Credit Card Payments
  1. Loan Payment  _____
  2. Loan Payment  _____
  3. Credit Card Payment  _____
  4. Credit Card Payment  _____
  5. Credit Card Payment  _____
  6. Credit Card Payment  _____
  7. Student Loan Payments  _____
  7. Miscellaneous Payments  _____
**Total Loan and Credit Card Payments**  _____

V.  Life and Disability Insurance Premiums
  1. Life Insurance Premiums  _____
  2. Disability Insurance Premiums  _____
    **Total Insurance Premiums**  _____

VI.  Taxes (Complete this section if you pay your taxes in quarterly estimates rather than through payroll deduction)
  1. Federal Income Tax  _____
  2. State Income Tax  _____
  3. Local Income Tax  _____
    **Total Taxes**  _____

VII.  Education
     1. Tuition          _____
     2. Other Related Expenses   _____
         **Total Education Expenses**   _____

VIII. Other           _____

**Totals of Expenses:**

|        |                                  |         |
|--------|----------------------------------|---------|
| I.     | Home                             | _____ |
| II.    | Living                           | _____ |
| III.   | Medical                          | _____ |
| IV.    | Installment Loan and Credit Card | _____ |
| V.     | Insurance Premiums               | _____ |
| VI.    | Taxes                            | _____ |
| VII.   | Education                        | _____ |
| VIII.  | Other                            | _____ |
|        | **Total Expenses**               | _____ |

**Total Income**   _____
**Minus Total Expenses**   _____
**Income Left After Expenses**   _____

# 3

# INSURANCE

---

Your objectives are to:
1. Prepare an inventory of your life insurance policies.
2. Determine if your beneficiary designations are up-to-date.
3. Prepare an inventory of the contents of your home(s).


## I. LIFE INSURANCE

### PREPARE AN INVENTORY OF POLICIES

Prepare an up-to-date inventory of your life insurance policies so that at your death, your spouse or loved ones will know where to file claims.

Turn to the perforated section at the end of the book and tear out the section titled "Life Insurance-Inventory." For each policy list the company name, the amount of the policy, and the names of the primary and secondary beneficiaries. Also record if the policy pays an accidental death benefit. Also include life insurance provided by your employer. (If your employer provides life insurance but you do not have an actual policy, label a folder "Life Insurance-Employer". Insert a sheet of paper in the folder on which you have listed the amount of the policy and the phone number of the office or department your spouse or loved one should contact after your death).

There may be other sources of life insurance to include on the inventory. For example:

- Life insurance policies issued by fraternal organizations and\or labor unions.
- Credit union loans that include a death benefit.
- Credit cards that pay a death benefit at the death of the card holder.

After you have completed the Life Insurance-Inventory, make a photocopy. Label a folder "Life Insurance (Date)" and place one copy of the inventory in the folder. Attach the other copy to your trust. If you do not have a trust, attach the copy to your will. Place the folders containing the life insurance policies and the Life Insurance-Inventory in alphabetical order in the file cabinet or storage box.

Update the Life Insurance-Inventory as often as necessary. To update the inventory, photocopy the form at the end of this chapter and fill in the information. After you have completed the updated inventory, make a photocopy. Insert one copy in the folder. Attach the other copy to your trust or will, discarding the out-of-date copy. Repeat this process each time you update the Life Insurance-Inventory.

## BENEFICIARY DESIGNATIONS

Life insurance benefits pass directly to the person or persons named as the beneficiaries without going through Probate. (Probate is discussed in Chapter 5.) Make certain that the person or persons listed as beneficiaries are the ones you want to receive the life insurance benefits at your death.

Have you named a secondary beneficiary? (also known as contingent beneficiary). A secondary or contingent beneficiary receives life insurance benefits if the primary beneficiary dies before you.

To change a primary beneficiary or a secondary beneficiary or to add a secondary beneficiary, file a "Change of Beneficiary" form with the insurance company. Call or write the company and request the form. After you have completed and signed the form, make a photocopy for your records and return the original to the company.

Request written confirmation from the company that they have received the change of beneficiary form. Attach your copy of the form and the confirmation from the insurance company to the insurance policy.

If you name your "estate" as the beneficiary, the insurance proceeds will go through probate and be distributed according to your will if you have a will or according to the laws of your state if you don't have a will (See Chapter 5).

## II. DISABILITY INSURANCE

Disability insurance protects against a loss of income due to a lengthy illness or a permanent disability. Assemble information about your disability insurance coverage. Review your coverage and make changes if necessary. If you do not have disability insurance, consider it.

Insert the disability insurance information into a folder. Label and file the folder.

## III. AUTO INSURANCE

Assemble information about your auto insurance. Review your coverage and make changes if necessary.

Insert the auto insurance information into a folder. Label and file the folder.

## IV. HOMEOWNER'S INSURANCE OR RENTER'S INSURANCE

Assemble information about your homeowner's or renter's insurance. Review your coverage and make changes if necessary.

Take the time to do a "Home Inventory." It will be invaluable in the event of fire or other major destruction.

**Home Inventory**

To prepare a home inventory, use a camera or video recorder and photograph or record **EVERY-THING** in your home including window treatments, floor coverings, lights and wall hangings. Open cabinets, closets, and drawers and photograph or record the contents. Include the basement, attic, garage, and other storage buildings.

On a sheet of paper, list the serial numbers of major items. Also gather receipts of major purchases. Receipts are useful because they include a description of the item, the date of purchase, and the cost.

Make a copy of the Home Inventory, serial numbers, and receipts and store them outside of your home i.e. in a safe deposit box or a secure location at your place of employment.

Insert the homeowner's insurance information, the list of serial numbers, and the receipts into a folder. Label and file the folder.

If you have a vacation home, prepare a vacation home inventory.

## V. HEALTH INSURANCE

Assemble information about your health insurance. Review your coverage and make changes if necessary.

Insert the health insurance information into a folder. Label and file the folder.

# CHECKLIST

## LIFE INSURANCE

### Prepare an Inventory of Life Insurance Policies

❏ Assemble information about each policy including:

* policies provided by employer,
* policies from fraternal organizations,
* policies from labor unions,
* benefits included in credit union loans,
* benefits paid by credit card companies.

❏ Review coverage, make changes as necessary.

❏ Tear out the "Life Insurance-Inventory" from the perforated section.

❏ List the company name, amount of policy, and primary and secondary beneficiaries.

❏ Photocopy the inventory.

❏ Label a folder "Life Insurance(Date)."

❏ Place one copy of the inventory in the folder.

❏ File the folder.

❏ Attach the other copy to your trust or will.

## Beneficiary Designation

- ❑ Check primary and secondary beneficiaries.
- ❑ Change as necessary.
- ❑ Contact company and request change of beneficiary form.
- ❑ Complete the form, sign it, make a copy for your records.
- ❑ Return the original to the company and request written confirmation.
- ❑ Attach the copy of the change of beneficiary form and the confirmation to the insurance policy.

## DISABILITY INSURANCE

- ❑ Assemble information about your disability insurance.
- ❑ Review your coverage and make changes as necessary.
- ❑ Insert the information into a folder. Label and file the folder.
- ❑ Consider disability insurance if you don't have it.

## AUTO INSURANCE

- ❑ Assemble information about your auto insurance.

❑ Review your coverage and make changes as necessary.

❑ Insert the information into a folder. Label and file the folder.

## HOMEOWNER'S OR RENTER'S INSURANCE

❑ Assemble information about your homeowners insurance.

❑ Review your coverage and make changes as necessary.

❑ Insert the information into a folder. Label and file the folder.

❑ Prepare a home inventory.

❑ Include serial numbers and receipts of major purchases.

❑ Prepare a home inventory of vacation property.

❑ Store copies outside your home.

## HEALTH INSURANCE

❑ Assemble information about your health insurance.

❑ Review your coverage and make changes as necessary.

❑ Insert the information into a folder. Label and file the folder.

## LIFE INSURANCE INVENTORY _____ (Date)

| Insured | Company | Amount | Accidental | Beneficiaries Primary | Secondary |
|---------|---------|--------|------------|----------------------|-----------|
|  |  |  |  |  |  |
|  |  |  |  |  |  |
|  |  |  |  |  |  |
|  |  |  |  |  |  |
|  |  |  |  |  |  |

# 4

# PENSIONS AND
# RETIREMENT PLANS

Your objectives are to:
1. Prepare an inventory of your pension and retirement plans.
2. Determine if your beneficiary designations are up-to-date.
3. Start planning for retirement if you have no plan.

## PREPARE AN INVENTORY OF PENSIONS AND RETIREMENT PLANS

This inventory will be an up-to-date record of your retirement plans and retirement accounts so that at your death your loved ones will know where to file claims.

Turn to the perforated section at the end of the book and tear out the section titled "Pension and Retirement-Inventory". Insert the date at the top. Consulting the information you accumulated about IRA accounts, Keogh accounts, pension/profit sharing plans, 401k(s), thrift savings, stock purchase, etc. (Chapter 1), list the company name, the amount in the retirement plan or account, and the names of the primary and secondary beneficiaries.

Photocopy the inventory. Label a folder "Retirement and Pension (Date)" and place a copy of the Pension and Retirement-Inventory in the folder. Attach the other copy to your trust. If you do not have a trust, attach the copy to your will.

Place the folders containing the pension and retirement information and the Retirement and Pension-Inventory in alphabetical order in the file cabinet or storage box.

To update the inventory, photocopy the Retirement and Pension-Inventory form at the end of this chapter and fill in the information. After completing the updated inventory make a photocopy. Insert one copy in the folder discarding the out-of-date inventory. Attach the other copy to your Trust or Will, discarding the out-of-date copy. Repeat this process each time you update the Pension and Retirement-Inventory.

## BENEFICIARY DESIGNATIONS

Retirement plans or accounts that allow you to designate a beneficiary will pass directly to the beneficiary without going through probate. (Probate is discussed in Chapter 5.) Make certain that the person or persons listed as beneficiaries are the ones you want to receive these benefits at your death.

Have you named a secondary beneficiary? (also

known as contingent beneficiary). A secondary or contingent beneficiary receives the retirement benefits if the primary beneficiary dies before you.

If you name a nonspouse as beneficiary, there will be tax consequences. Seek competent tax advice if you plan to name a nonspouse as a beneficiary or if you have any questions about the tax implications of your retirement plan.

## REVIEW YOUR PLAN FOR RETIREMENT

Regardless of how far in the future retirement seems at the moment, at some point you will want to retire. The sooner you start planning for your retirement, the better prepared you will be.

How you actually plan for retirement is beyond the scope of this book. Seek the advice of a competent financial planner.

## SOCIAL SECURITY INCOME ESTIMATE

An important part of any retirement planning is an accurate estimate of the social security income you will receive at retirement. The Social Security Administration will mail you a free personalized accounting of your payments into Social Security and the income you can expect to receive when eligible.

Call 1-800-937-2700 and request Form SA 7004 entitled "Request for Earnings and Benefit Estimate

Statement." Follow the instructions included with the form.

When you receive the Request for Earnings and Benefit Estimate Statement, review it carefully. If you find that the Administration has made an error in recording your past payments, correct this error promptly to avoid problems in the future.

# CHECKLIST

❑ Assemble information about your retirement plans.

❑ Tear out "Pension and Retirement-Inventory" from the perforated section.

❑ List retirement plans, pension plans, IRAs etc., the amount in the plan or account and the primary and secondary beneficiaries.

❑ Review your beneficiaries and make changes as necessary.

❑ Review your overall plan for retirement and makes changes as necessary.

❑ Begin planning NOW if you do not have a retirement plan.

❑ Call 1-800-937-2700 and request Form SA 7004.

❑ Review the Request for Earnings and Benefit Estimate Statement for accuracy. Make corrections as necessary.

# PENSION AND RETIREMENT PLANS

## PENSION AND RETIREMENT INVENTORY _____ (Date)

| Plan\Account | Amount | Beneficiaries | |
|---|---|---|---|
| | | Primary | Secondary |
| | | | |
| | | | |
| | | | |
| | | | |
| | | | |
| | | | |
| | | | |

# 5

# LEGAL AFFAIRS
# ESTATE PLANNING

---

**Estate planning** is planning for the management of your assets (your estate) during your lifetime and the distribution of your assets (your estate) at your death.

Your objectives as you work through Chapter 5 are to:

1. Understand how to appoint someone to act for you if you become disabled or incompetent.
2. Understand how assets are transferred at your death.
3. Understand the amount you can transfer by lifetime gifts or at death without paying gift or estate taxes.
4. Determine your estate planning objectives.
5. Determine if your estate plan meets your objectives.
6. Make changes in your estate plan if it does not meet your objectives.

7. Develop and implement an estate plan if you do not already have one.

## PLANNING FOR THE MANAGEMENT OF YOUR ASSETS IF YOU BECOME DISABLED OR INCOMPETENT

You can appoint a spouse, loved one, or trusted friend to manage your assets if you become disabled or incompetent by using a power of attorney or a living trust.

### I. Power of Attorney

A Power of Attorney is a legal document which authorizes the person you select to act as your agent should you become disabled or incompetent.

If you become disabled or incompetent you may need an agent to manage your assets, pay your bills, and\or to make medical decisions for you.

You can appoint a spouse, loved one, or trusted friend to act for you as your agent. The Power of Attorney will take effect either at the time you sign the document or at the time you become incompetent. Be sure to discuss these options with your attorney.

### Three Important Points about Powers of Attorney:

1. You cannot legally sign a Power of Attorney if you are incompetent. Therefore, it is necessary to

have signed a Power of Attorney before becoming incompetent.

2. Name an alternate in case the first person you name in the Power of Attorney is not available or able to act.

3. A Power of Attorney terminates at your death.

## II. Living Trust

A Living Trust is an agreement between the trust maker and the trustee for the benefit of the beneficiaries named in the trust. **Generally** you are the trust maker, you are the initial trustee, and you are the initial beneficiary.

You, as the trustee, manage the trust assets during your lifetime. You, as the beneficiary, receive trust income and principal during your lifetime. At your death your successor trustee distributes the assets to the persons you have designated as your successor beneficiaries.

You remain trustee unless you resign or become incompetent, at which time the successor trustee you named in the trust takes over. The successor trustee can be your spouse, family member, friend, or a financial institution.

A living trust is useful if you become disabled or incompetent because a successor trustee is authorized to take over the management of the trust assets during your disability or incompetency. Even if your successor takes over as trustee, the trust income and principal is still used for your care and support.

## APPOINTING A TRUSTED INDIVIDUAL TO MAKE DECISIONS CONCERNING YOUR MEDICAL CARE

A medical power of attorney appoints a spouse, loved one, or other trusted individual to make medical decisions for you if you become incapacitated or incompetent. A medical power of attorney is also known as a health care proxy and a patient advocate designation.

A living will is a document in which you express your wishes concerning the use of life-support treatment.

You cannot legally sign a medical power of attorney or a living will if you are incompetent. Therefore, it is necessary to have signed these documents before becoming incompetent.

## PLANNING FOR THE DISTRIBUTION OF YOUR ASSETS AT DEATH

To plan for the distribution of your assets at your death, you need to understand:

1. How assets are transferred from one person to another; and
2. When a probate court is involved in the transfer.

Assets are transferred at death either by: beneficiary designation, joint ownership, will, intestacy, or trust.

## 1. Beneficiary Designation

Certain types of assets permit you to name beneficiaries who will receive the asset at your death. You can appoint one or more primary beneficiaries and one or more secondary beneficiaries. Secondary beneficiaries are also called contingent beneficiaries.

At your death, the person or persons you have named as your primary beneficiary will receive the asset. If all of your primary beneficiaries are deceased, the person or persons you have named as your secondary beneficiary will receive the asset.

Examples of assets that permit you to name beneficiaries are: life insurance policies, annuities, IRAs, certain types of retirement plans, certain types of bank accounts, and certain types of brokerage accounts.

Assets that are transferred by beneficiary designation avoid probate court. However, if all of the beneficiaries you have named die before you, the asset will pass through probate court.

If you have assets that permit you to name beneficiaries, review your beneficiary designations. If changes are necessary, take action now.

To change a primary beneficiary or a secondary beneficiary or to add a secondary beneficiary, file a "Change of Beneficiary" form with the company. Call or write the company and request the form. After you have completed and signed the form, make a photocopy for your records and return the original to the company. Request written confirmation from the company that they have received the form. Attach the change of beneficiary form and the confirmation to the policy, annuity, etc.

## 2. Joint Ownership

An asset which is titled in your name and the name of another person(s) as "joint tenants with rights of survivorship" will transfer to the surviving joint tenant(s) at your death without passing through probate court.

However, if none of the joint tenants survive you, the asset must pass through probate court and will be distributed according to your will. If you do not have a will, the asset must still pass through probate court and will be distributed according to the laws of intestacy.(Section 4 below).

The advantage of joint ownership with rights of survivorship is that it avoids probate court.

The disadvantages of joint ownership with rights of survivorship are:

- You must have the joint tenants' cooperation and participation to sell the asset.
- The asset is vulnerable to the joint tenants' lawsuits, creditors, and divorce.

### 3. Will

If assets are transferred by will, **THE ASSETS MUST PASS THROUGH PROBATE COURT**. The preceding sentence may surprise you as most people believe that if they have a will they have avoided probate court. However, that belief is incorrect.

The purpose of a will is to tell the probate court who is to receive the assets, who is to administer the probate estate (that person is either called a personal representative or an executor), and who is to be the guardian of minor children.

### 4. Intestacy-No Will

If, at your death, there are assets in your name only and you do not have a will, your assets must still pass through probate court. In this situation your assets will be distributed to the persons designated by the laws of your state. Generally, state laws designate the closest family members to receive the assets of a person who dies without a will.

### 5. Living Trust

A Living Trust is an agreement between the trust maker and the trustee for the benefit of the beneficiaries named in the trust. **Generally,** you are the trust maker, you are the initial trustee, and you are the initial beneficiary.

You, as the trustee, manage the trust assets during your lifetime. You, as the beneficiary, receive trust income and principal during your lifetime. At your death, your successor trustee distributes the assets to the persons you have designated as your successor beneficiaries.

You remain trustee unless you resign or become incompetent, at which time the successor trustee you named in the trust takes over. The successor trustee can be your spouse, family member, friend, or a financial institution.

At your death, if your assets are in the name of your trust, the assets will be transferred directly to the beneficiaries you have named in the trust, and probate court is avoided.

However, if you have a living trust but have not transferred your assets to the name of your trust, the assets must first pass through probate court before they will be transferred to your beneficiaries.

You transfer assets to your trust by changing the title of the asset from your name to the name of your trust. If you have a trust but your assets have not been transferred to the trust, contact your attorney immediately.

## SUMMARY: TRANSFERRING ASSETS WITHOUT PROBATE COURT

You will avoid probate if:

1. Your assets pass by beneficiary designation and the beneficiary survives you.

2. You hold title to the assets as joint tenant with rights of survivorship and your joint tenant survives you.
3. You have a living trust and all of your assets are in the name of your trust.

## SUMMARY: TRANSFERRING ASSETS THROUGH PROBATE COURT

Any asset that is titled in your name alone must pass through probate court regardless of whether or not you have a will.

## GIFT AND ESTATE TAXES

Before January 1, 1998, each person could transfer up to $600,000 by lifetime gifts or at death without paying gift or estate taxes. After January 1, 1998, the amount exempt from gift and estate taxes gradually increases so that by the year 2006 each person can transfer up to $1,000,000 by lifetime gifts or at death without paying taxes. A married couple, with proper estate planning, will be able to pass up to $2,000,000 by lifetime gifts or at death without paying federal gift or estate taxes.

| Graduated Schedule | |
|---|---|
| **Year** | **Amount That Passes Tax Free** |
| 1998 | $625,000 |
| 1999 | $650,000 |

| | |
|---|---|
| 2000-01 | $675,000 |
| 2002-03 | $700,000 |
| 2004 | $850,000 |
| 2005 | $950,000 |
| 2006 | $1,000,000 |

## WHAT ARE YOUR ESTATE PLANNING OBJECTIVES?

There are many possible objectives:

1. The orderly transfer of your assets to the person(s) you select.
2. Eliminating or reducing estate taxes.
3. Avoiding probate court.
4. Naming a guardian for minor children.
5. Planning for children or adults with special needs.
6. Appointing a trusted individual to act on your behalf in the event of disability or incompetency.
7. Appointing a trusted individual to make medical decisions for you if you are incapable or unable to make decisions yourself.

## DOES YOUR EXISTING PLAN MEET YOUR OBJECTIVES?

Once you have listed your objectives in the order of their priority, determine if your existing estate plan meets your objectives. If not, contact your attorney and revise your estate plan.

## WHAT IF YOU DO NOT HAVE AN ESTATE PLAN?

Determine your objectives. Then consult an attorney who specializes in estate planning and formulate and implement a plan that meets your objectives.

## THE STORAGE OF YOUR ESTATE PLAN DOCUMENTS

Make copies of your estate plan documents. Store the **original** documents in a safe place, i.e. safe deposit box. Store the copies in a folder. Label and file the folder.

# CHECKLIST

❑ Have you planned for the management of your assets and the payment of your bills if you become disabled or incompetent?

❑ Have you planned for a trusted individual to make medical decisions for you if you are unable to make them yourself?

❑ Have you planned for the distribution of your assets at your death?

❑ Have you appointed a guardian for your minor children?

❑ Does your estate plan meet your objectives?

❑ Make changes in your estate plan if it does not meet your objectives. Consult your attorney.

❑ Develop and implement an estate plan if you do not already have one. Consult an experienced estate planning attorney.

❑ Store the original documents in a safe place.

# 6

# CREDIT CARDS AND CREDIT HISTORY

Your objectives are to:
1. Prepare an inventory of your credit cards.
2. Review your credit history.
3. Prepare an inventory of the contents of your wallet.

## WHY PREPARE AN INVENTORY OF CREDIT CARDS?

An inventory of your credit cards will be invaluable if your credit cards are lost or stolen. You will be able to contact the credit card companies quickly and efficiently by using the information included on the inventory.

The inventory will also remind you of the number of credit cards you have and the interest rate and yearly fees charged by each credit card company.

## HOW TO PREPARE A CREDIT CARD INVENTORY

Tear out the "Credit Card-Inventory" from the perforated section. Using your credit card statements or other information provided by the credit card companies, record the card name, card number, the phone number to call if the credit card is lost or stolen, the interest rate and the annual fee, if any.

Evaluate whether or not you could or should eliminate one or more cards. If so, contact the company in writing. Keep a copy of your letter for your records. Destroy the card(s).

Label a folder "Credit Cards(Date)", insert the inventory and copies of any correspondence to the credit card companies.

To update the inventory, photocopy the Credit Card-Inventory form at the end of this chapter and fill in the information. Insert the updated inventory in the folder and discard the out-of-date inventory.

## CREDIT HISTORY

Your credit history is checked every time you apply for a loan or a line of credit, so your credit history must be accurate.

There are three major agencies that provide credit reports, Experian (formerly TRW), Trans Union Corporation and Equifax. As each agency keeps separate records, their credit reports may differ. So it's wise to review each agency's report. If you are married, both you and your spouse should review your credit reports.

If you find mistakes in your credit report take steps to correct the mistakes immediately. Otherwise future credit applications may be denied.

To order a credit report call Experian at 800-682-7654, Trans Union Corporation at 800-888-4213 and Equifax at 800-685-1111.

## WOMEN AND CREDIT

If you are married and have not established a credit history in your name, you may find it difficult to obtain credit after the death of your husband. If you don't have a credit history, take steps to establish credit in your name.

Apply for a credit card in your name only. Make monthly purchases using the credit card and pay the balance in full **ON TIME**. Use the credit card even if you would prefer to pay by cash or check. Otherwise you will not establish a credit history of your own.

## PREPARE AN INVENTORY OF THE CONTENTS OF YOUR WALLET

Prepare an inventory of the contents of your wallet. Tear out "Contents of Wallet" from the perforated section. List the contents of your wallet. Label a folder "Wallet Contents" and insert the inventory in the folder.

# CHECKLIST

❑ Prepare an inventory of your credit cards.

❑ Request credit reports from Experian, Trans Union Corporation and Equifax.

❑ Review the reports from accuracy.

❑ Correct any mistakes.

❑ Prepare an inventory of the contents of your wallet.

# CREDIT CARD-INVENTORY _____

| Company | Account Number | Phone No | Interest Rate | Fee |
|---------|----------------|----------|---------------|-----|
|         |                |          |               |     |
|         |                |          |               |     |
|         |                |          |               |     |
|         |                |          |               |     |
|         |                |          |               |     |
|         |                |          |               |     |

# CONTENTS OF WALLET (Date)

_____

_____

_____

_____

_____

_____

_____

# 7

# TAXES

Your objectives are to:
1. Locate your income tax returns from prior years.
2. Set up a system to collect and organize the information that will be needed to file future income tax returns.

## LOCATE TAX RETURNS FROM PRIOR YEARS

If, because of disability, you are unable to file federal, state, and local income tax returns, your spouse, loved one, or a trusted friend will have to file them for you. Your tax returns from prior years are a good place for them to start.

Locate your federal, state, and local tax returns for the past three years. Insert each year's returns in a separate folder and label the folders (i.e. "Tax Returns 1997").

File the folders in chronological order in your file cabinet or storage box.

# DEVELOP A SYSTEM TO COLLECT AND ORGANIZE INFORMATION FOR FUTURE TAX RETURNS

Whether you or someone else will be preparing your income tax returns, streamline the process by having the information about each year's income and deductions accessible and organized.

## INCOME EARNED DURING THE YEAR

Label a separate folder for each type of income you earn or receive during the year. Insert the information as it's received throughout the year in the appropriate folder. If an income has closely related expenses, file the information about the income and the expenses in the same folder.

**Sources of income:**
- Wage and salary ( W-2).
- Interest income (1099-INT).
- Dividend income (1099-DIV).
- Seller-financed mortgage interest income.
- Business income (and expenses).
- Sales of stocks, securities and installment sales (1099-A) (1099-B) (1099-S).
- Sale, exchange or purchase of real estate. Sales of personal residence (include fixing-up expenses, expenses associated with selling your home and moving expenses).

- Rental income (and expenses).
- Royalty income.
- Income from pensions and annuities (1099-R).
- Partnerships, S Corporations, estates and trusts (K-1 schedules).
- Farm income (and expenses).
- Unemployment compensation.
- Social Security benefits.
- Railroad retirement benefits.
- IRA distributions.
- Alimony.
- IRA, Keogh, SEP, and SIMPLE contributions.

## ASSETS SOLD DURING THE YEAR

You will also need to collect and organize specific information about the assets you sold during the year. Consulting the information you accumulated about your assets and debts (Chapter 1) record:

- the date the asset was purchased,
- the purchase price,
- the date the asset was sold, and
- the sales price.

## GIFTS

Did you make gifts of more than $10,000 to any one individual during the year? If so, inform your tax advisor.

## DEDUCTIONS ITEMIZED AND MISCELLANEOUS

Label a separate folder for each type of deduction. Insert the information as it's received throughout the year in the appropriate folder. For example:

- Medical and dental expenses.
- Taxes (real estate and personal property).
- Mortgage interest.
- Home equity interest.
- Investment interest.
- Alimony paid.
- Charitable contributions.
- Child and dependent care expenses.
- Union and professional dues.
- Tax preparation fee.
- Safe deposit box.
- Unreimbursed employee business expenses.
- Certain legal and accounting fees.
- Casualty and theft losses.

## FILING SYSTEM

Allocate a section of your file cabinet or storage box for the folders which contain tax preparation information. File the folders in alphabetical order.

As soon as you have all the necessary information, schedule a meeting with your tax advisor (or prepare the tax returns yourself). File the returns and place copies in a folder labeled "Tax Returns (Year)".

Start the process again and collect and organize the information you will need to prepare next year's income tax returns.

Contact your tax advisor any time you have questions or concerns. By doing so, you will resolve minor problems before they become major ones.

# CHECKLIST

**TAXES**

1. Locate tax returns from prior years and insert them in folders.

2. Collect and organize information about the year's income.

Sources of income:
- Wage and salary ( W-2).
- Interest income (1099-INT).
- Dividend income (1099-DIV).
- Seller-financed mortgage interest income.
- Business income (and expenses).
- Sales of stocks, securities and installment sales (1099-A) (1099-B) (1099-S).
- Sale, exchange or purchase of real estate.
- Sales of personal residence (include fixing-up expenses, expenses associated with selling your home and moving expenses).
- Rental income (and expenses).
- Royalty income.
- Income from pensions and annuities (1099-R).
- Partnerships, S Corporations, estates and trusts (K-1 schedules).
- Farm income (and expenses).

- Unemployment compensation.
- Social Security benefits.
- Railroad retirement benefits.
- IRA distributions.
- Alimony.
- IRA, Keogh, SEP, and SIMPLE contributions.

3. Collect and organize information about the year's deductions.

For example:
- Medical and dental expenses.
- Taxes (real estate and personal property).
- Mortgage interest.
- Home equity interest.
- Investment interest.
- Alimony paid.
- Charitable contributions.
- Child and dependent care expenses.
- Union and professional dues.
- Tax preparation fee.
- Safe deposit box.
- Unreimbursed employee business expenses.
- Certain legal and accounting fees.
- Casualty and theft losses.

# 8

# KEEPING YOUR FINANCIAL AND LEGAL AFFAIRS UP-TO-DATE

---

Now that your financial and legal affairs are in order, plan to keep them up-to-date.

## PERIODIC REVIEWS

Schedule periodic reviews of:

- assets and debts,
- income and expenses,
- insurance policies,
- pension\retirement plans,
- estate plan,
- credit, and
- tax matters.

Review these issues yearly **and** when events alter your financial and\or legal circumstances. Examples of events that should prompt a review are: marriage or remarriage, birth, divorce, death, employment changes, retirement, and the purchase or sale of significant assets.

## WHEN TO SCHEDULE REVIEWS

Develop a sensible review schedule. For example, review your retirement plans and tax matters in early December so that you have time to make adjustments before year end. Review assets and debts, income and expenses, credit matters, and your estate plan just before or just after you file your yearly tax returns.

Schedule a review of your homeowner's insurance coverage and your home inventory a month before the next premium is due. Schedule a review of your auto insurance coverage a month before the next premium is due.

## HOW TO SCHEDULE REVIEWS

Incorporate periodic reviews of your financial and legal matters into your weekly planner or diary system. If you do not use a planner or diary, use your kitchen calendar or the pocket calendar you carry in your purse or briefcase. Write a brief description of the matter to be reviewed at the date that is most appropriate for the review. Check your calendar regularly.

**Being reminded to review a specific financial or legal matter is useless if you do not actually review the matter and then make the necessary changes.**

# 9

# LOCATION OF DOCUMENTS AND OTHER INFORMATION

Your objectives are to:
1. Provide information about the location of your important documents.
2. Provide information about your doctors, other health personnel and medications.
3. Provide information about the people to contact in an emergency.
4. Provide information about your financial and legal advisors.
5. Provide information about a pre-arranged funeral and\or burial.

## COMPLETE THE LISTS AND MAKE THEM ACCESSIBLE TO YOUR LOVED ONES

Turn to Chapter 9 in the perforated section and tear out the lists that apply to you. Fill in the information and then place the lists in a safe but accessible place. Tell your loved ones where they will find the information and make certain they will be able to gain access. For example, if you place the lists in your safe deposit box, be sure your loved ones know where the box is and give them a key.

You may prefer to make a copy of the lists and give the copy directly to your loved one.

## UPDATE THE INFORMATION

To update the information, make a photocopy of the lists that appear at the end of this chapter. Fill in the information. Replace the out of date lists with the updated ones. Discard the out-of-date lists.

## A FINAL SUGGESTION

Now that you have your financial and legal affairs in order are there personal or family matters that need your attention? If so, why not take action now. Good luck and take care.

# LOCATION OF IMPORTANT DOCUMENTS

**Item**                                    **Location**

Will_____

Trust  _____

Power of attorney _____

Medical power of attorney_____

Living will  _____


Asset\debt information (Attach Inventory)

Property deeds  _____

Other real estate documents  _____

Savings bonds  _____

Certificates of deposit, T-Bills  _____

Stock certificates  _____

Promissory notes_____

Limited partnerships  _____


Insurance policies (Attach Inventory)

Home Inventory  _____

Vacation Home Inventory  _____


Pension, IRA, Keogh, 401(k) records

(Attach Inventory)  _____

Employee benefit documents  _____

Automobile  _____

**LOCATION OF DOCUMENTS AND OTHER INFORMATION**

Other vehicle\boats title\registrations _____

Birth certificates _____

Death certificates _____

Marriage license _____

Military discharge papers _____

Passport_____

Tax returns _____

Credit Card Inventory (Attach Inventory) _____

Any other legal documents _____

# BANKS AND CREDIT UNIONS

Bank and Address

_____

_____

_____

_____

_____

# SAFE DEPOSIT BOX

| Bank and Address | Number | Who Has Access | Location of Key |
|---|---|---|---|
| _____ | _____ | _____ | _____ |
| _____ | _____ | _____ | _____ |
| _____ | _____ | _____ | _____ |
| _____ | _____ | _____ | _____ |

## MEDICAL INFORMATION

Doctors
Name                    Phone              Address

_____    _____    _____

_____    _____    _____

_____    _____    _____

_____    _____    _____

_____    _____    _____


Other Health Personnel
Name and Title          Phone              Address

_____    _____    _____

_____    _____    _____

_____    _____    _____


Current Medications
Medication              Dose               Pharmacy

_____    _____    _____

_____    _____    _____

_____    _____    _____

_____    _____    _____

## CONTACT IN AN EMERGENCY

| Name | Relationship | Phone | Address |
|------|-------------|-------|---------|
|      |             |       |         |
|      |             |       |         |
|      |             |       |         |
|      |             |       |         |
|      |             |       |         |
|      |             |       |         |
|      |             |       |         |
|      |             |       |         |

## FAMILY ADVISORS

Financial Advisor
Stock Broker
Name, Firm, Phone                    Address

_____    _____

_____    _____

_____    _____

Accountant
Name, Firm, Phone                    Address

_____    _____

_____    _____

Attorney
Name, Firm, Phone                    Address

_____    _____

_____    _____

Insurance Agent
Name, Firm,Phone                    Address

_____    _____

_____    _____

## FUNERAL ARRANGEMENTS

Name of Funeral Home _____

Address _____

Phone _____

Location of Contract _____

Date of Contract _____

Arrangements _____

_____

_____

_____

## BURIAL ARRANGEMENTS

Name of Cemetery or place of Burial _____

Address _____

Phone _____

Location of Contract _____

Date of Contract _____

Arrangements _____

_____

_____

_____

# CHECKLISTS

# CHAPTER 1

**Establish A Record Storage Area:**

**"Shopping List":**

❑ a large box of legal size manila folders

❑ a legal size metal file cabinet, or

❑ 12" by 18" storage box with cover.

**Information To Locate**

❑ Identification Numbers:
* social security
* military service
* driver's license
* health insurance number
* children's social security numbers
* other important numbers.

❑ Tax returns.

❑ Will, trust, trust amendments, power of attorney, medical power of attorney and living will. (**Make copies of these documents. Return the originals to a safe place and store the copies in the folders.)**

82

❏ Military discharge papers.

❏ Insurance policies.

❏ Birth certificates for all family members.

❏ Marriage license.

❏ Up-to-date information about each of your assets and debts.

❏ Pension or retirement plans.

❏ Real estate closing or escrow papers.

❏ "Buy-Sell Agreement" and other business ownership documents.

❏ Divorce Judgment or decree, if divorced.

❏ Name, address, and phone number of physician and other health personnel.

❏ Name, address, and phone number of accountant, attorney, financial planner, insurance agent, and other current advisors.

❏ Preplanned funeral, and burial information.

Store the folders in alphabetical order in the file cabinet or storage box.

## Records Stored On Computer

❏ **Make backup copies of computer records.**

❏ **Prepare a set of instructions so loved ones can access the information stored on your computer.**

# CHAPTER 2

## Inventory of Assets and Debts

❑ Record the value of each asset and each debt on the inventory located in the perforated section.

❑ Record the name or names on the title of the asset.

❑ Determine if each asset is correctly titled.

❑ If changes are necessary, take action immediately.

❑ Place the labeled folders in alphabetical order in the file cabinet or storage box.

❑ Label a folder "Inventory (Year)," make a photocopy of the inventory and insert one copy in this folder.

❑ Attach the other copy to your trust or will.

## Update the Inventory

❑ Update the Inventory yearly **AND** when you buy and sell assets, and incur or payoff large debts.

❑ Photocopy the inventory located at the end of Chapter 2 and insert the date.

❑ Record the value of each asset and each debt.

❑ Label another folder "Inventory (Year)."

❑ Make a copy of the updated inventory.

❑ Insert one copy in the folder and attach the other to your trust or will. Discard the out-of-date inventory.

# INVENTORY _____ (Date)

## ASSETS

| Type of Asset | Current Value of Asset | How Asset is Titled (Name, Names or Trust Name on title) | |
|---|---|---|---|
| **I.  Cash Assets** | | **Value** | **Title** |
| 1.  Cash on hand | | _____ | _____ |
| 2.  Checking Account(s) (Bank and Credit Union) | | | |
| | | _____ | _____ |
| | | _____ | _____ |
| | | _____ | _____ |
| 3.  Savings accounts (Bank and Credit Union) | | | |
| | | _____ | _____ |
| | | _____ | _____ |
| | | _____ | _____ |
| 4.  Money Market account(s) | | _____ | _____ |
| | | _____ | _____ |
| **TOTAL CASH ASSETS** | | _____ | |

**II.   Investment Assets**               **Value**      **Title**

1.   Certificate(s) of Deposit          _____      _____

2.   Treasury Bills                      _____      _____

3.   Stocks (List the company, number of shares and
     current price per share)

| Company | Shares | Price Per Share | Total | Title |
|---------|--------|-----------------|-------|-------|
| \_\_\_\_\_ | \_\_\_\_\_ | \_\_\_\_\_ | \_\_\_\_\_ | \_\_\_\_\_ |
| \_\_\_\_\_ | \_\_\_\_\_ | \_\_\_\_\_ | \_\_\_\_\_ | \_\_\_\_\_ |
| \_\_\_\_\_ | \_\_\_\_\_ | \_\_\_\_\_ | \_\_\_\_\_ | \_\_\_\_\_ |
| \_\_\_\_\_ | \_\_\_\_\_ | \_\_\_\_\_ | \_\_\_\_\_ | \_\_\_\_\_ |

Total Value of Stocks      _____

4. Mutual Funds (List the fund, number of shares and current price per share)

| Fund | Shares | Price Per Share | Total | Title |
|------|--------|-----------------|-------|-------|
| _____ | \_\_\_\_\_ | _____ | _____ | \_\_\_\_\_ |
| _____ | \_\_\_\_\_ | _____ | _____ | \_\_\_\_\_ |
| _____ | \_\_\_\_\_ | _____ | _____ | \_\_\_\_\_ |
| _____ | \_\_\_\_\_ | _____ | _____ | \_\_\_\_\_ |

Total Value of Mutual Funds    _____

5.    U.S. Savings Bonds    _____    _____

6.    Municipal Bonds    _____    _____

7.    Corporate Bonds    _____    _____

**TOTAL INVESTMENT ASSETS**    _____

| **III.** | **Real Estate** | **Value** | **Title** |
|------|-----------------|-----------|-----------|
| 1. | Residence | _____ | _____ |
| 2. | Vacation Home | _____ | _____ |
| 3. | Vacant Land | _____ | _____ |

**Total of Real Estate Assets**    _____

**IV. Retirement/Pension/ Profit Sharing**

| | | Value | Title |
|---|---|---|---|
| 1. | IRA Accounts | _____ | _____ |
| 2. | Keogh Accounts | _____ | _____ |
| 3. | Pension/Profit Sharing Plans, 401(k), Thrift Savings, Stock Purchase | _____ | _____ |

**Total of Retirement/Pension/ Profit Sharing** _____

**V. Miscellaneous**

| | | Value | Title |
|---|---|---|---|
| 1. | Limited Partnerships | _____ | _____ |
| 2. | Notes, Mortgages or Other Debts Owed To You | _____ | _____ |
| 3. | Other | _____ | _____ |
| | | _____ | _____ |
| | | _____ | _____ |

**Total of Miscellaneous Assets** _____

**VI. Business Ownership** _____ _____

**VII. Vehicles\Boats**     **Value**     **Title**

| | | |
|---|---|---|
| _____ | _____ | _____ |
| _____ | _____ | _____ |
| _____ | _____ | _____ |

## Totals of Assets:

I.     Cash     _____

II.    Investment Assets     _____

III.   Real Estate Assets     _____

IV.   Retirement Assets     _____

V.    Miscellaneous Assets     _____

VI.   Business Ownership Assets     _____

VII.  Vehicles\Boats     _____

### TOTAL VALUE OF ALL ASSETS     _____

## DEBTS (LIABILITIES)

| Type of Debt | Current Balance |
|---|---|
| 1.  Mortgage (Residence) | _____ |
| 2.  Mortgage (Vacation Home) | _____ |
| 3.  Home Equity Loan | _____ |
| 4.  Auto Loan | _____ |
| 5.  Auto Loan | _____ |
| 6.  Credit Card | _____ |
| 7.  Credit Card | _____ |
| 8.  Credit Card | _____ |
| 9.  Student Loan | _____ |
| 9.  Life Insurance Loan | _____ |
| 10.  Other Loan(s) | _____ |
| **Total Debt** | _____ |

## NET WORTH:

**TOTAL VALUE OF ALL ASSETS** _____

**MINUS YOUR TOTAL DEBT** _____

**YOUR NET WORTH IS** _____

# INCOME AND EXPENSES
## INCOME

| Income | Amount Received Each Month |
|---|---|
| 1. Salary | _____ |
| 2. Social Security | _____ |
| 3. Pension-Retirement Benefits | _____ |
| 4. Annuity Payments | _____ |
| 5. Rental Income | _____ |
| 6. Interest | _____ |
| 7. Dividends | _____ |
| 8. Child Support | _____ |
| 9. Other | _____ |
| **Total Income** | _____ |

## EXPENSES

| Expense | Amount of Monthly Expense |
|---|---|
| I. Home | |
| 1. Mortgage or Rent | _____ |
| 2. Home Equity Loan Payment | _____ |
| 3. Property Taxes | _____ |
| 4. Insurance | _____ |
| 5. Association Dues | _____ |
| 6. Utilities | _____ |
| a. Heating Fuel | _____ |
| b. Gas | _____ |
| c. Electric | _____ |
| d. Water and Sewer | _____ |
| e. Telephone | _____ |

f. Cable TV _____
7. Repairs _____
   **Total Home Expenses** _____

II. Living
 1. Food _____
 2. Clothing _____
 3. Child Care _____
 4. Transportation
    a. Auto Loan Payment _____
    b. Auto Lease Payment _____
    c. Auto Insurance _____
    d. Gas and Oil _____
    e. Repairs _____
    f. Commuting expenses _____
 5. Pet Care _____
 6. Entertainment _____
   **Total Living Expenses** _____

III. Medical
 1. Health Insurance Premiums _____
 2. Dental Insurance Premiums _____
 3. Medicare Payments _____
 4. Doctor Visits _____
 5. Dental Care _____
 6. Eyeglasses _____
 7. Prescriptions _____
 8. Medical Supplies _____
 8. Miscellaneous Medical Expenses _____
   **Total Medical Expenses** _____

IV.   Loans (other than mortgage and home equity loans) and Credit Card Payments
   1. Loan Payment          _____
   2. Loan Payment          _____
   3. Credit Card Payment   _____
   4. Credit Card Payment   _____
   5. Credit Card Payment   _____
   6. Credit Card Payment   _____
   7. Student Loan Payments _____
   7. Miscellaneous Payments _____
   **Total Loan and Credit Card Payments**   _____

V.    Life and Disability Insurance Premiums
   1. Life Insurance Premiums        _____
   2. Disability Insurance Premiums  _____
       **Total Insurance Premiums**   _____

VI.   Taxes (Complete this section if you pay your taxes in quarterly estimates rather than through payroll deduction)
   1. Federal Income Tax   _____
   2. State Income Tax     _____
   3. Local Income Tax     _____
                **Total Taxes**   _____
VII.  Education
   1. Tuition                _____
   2. Other Related Expenses _____
        **Total Education Expenses**   _____

VIII. Other          _____

## Totals of Expenses:

I. Home                        _____

II. Living                      _____

III. Medical                  _____

IV. Installment Loan and Credit Card    _____

V. Insurance Premiums         _____

VI. Taxes                     _____

VII. Education               _____

VIII. Other                   _____

**Total Expenses**   _____

**Total Income**   _____

**Minus Total Expenses**   _____

**Income Left After Expenses**   _____

# CHAPTER 3

## LIFE INSURANCE

### Prepare an Inventory of Life Insurance Policies

❑ Assemble information about each policy including:

* policies provided by employer,
* policies from fraternal organizations,
* policies from labor unions,
* benefits included in credit union loans,
* benefits paid by credit card companies.

❑ Review coverage, make changes as necessary.

❑ Tear out the "Life Insurance-Inventory" from the perforated section.

❑ List the company name, amount of policy, and primary and secondary beneficiaries.

❑ Photocopy the inventory.

❑ Label a folder "Life Insurance(Date)."

❑ Place one copy of the inventory in the folder.

❑ File the folder.

❑ Attach the other copy to your trust or will.

## Beneficiary Designation

❏ Check primary and secondary beneficiaries.

❏ Change as necessary.

❏ Contact company and request change of beneficiary form.

❏ Complete the form, sign it, make a copy for your records.

❏ Return the original to the company and request written confirmation.

❏ Attach the copy of the change of beneficiary form and the confirmation to the insurance policy.

## DISABILITY INSURANCE

❏ Assemble information about your disability insurance.

❏ Review your coverage and make changes as necessary.

❏ Insert the information into a folder. Label and file the folder.

❏ Consider disability insurance if you don't have it.

## AUTO INSURANCE

❏ Assemble information about your auto insurance.

❑ Review your coverage and make changes as necessary.

❑ Insert the information into a folder. Label and file the folder.

## HOMEOWNER'S OR RENTER'S INSURANCE

❑ Assemble information about your homeowners insurance.

❑ Review your coverage and make changes as necessary.

❑ Insert the information into a folder. Label and file the folder.

❑ Prepare a home inventory.

❑ Include serial numbers and receipts of major purchases.

❑ Prepare a home inventory of vacation property.

❑ Store copies outside your home.

## HEALTH INSURANCE

❑ Assemble information about your health insurance.

❑ Review your coverage and make changes as necessary.

❑ Insert the information into a folder. Label and file the folder.

## LIFE INSURANCE INVENTORY _____(DATE)

| Insured | Company | Amount | Accidental | Beneficiaries | |
|---|---|---|---|---|---|
| | | | | Primary | Secondary |
| | | | | | |
| | | | | | |
| | | | | | |
| | | | | | |
| | | | | | |
| | | | | | |

# CHAPTER 4

❏ Assemble information about your retirement plans.

❏ Tear out "Pension and Retirement-Inventory" from the perforated section.

❏ List retirement plans, pension plans, IRAs etc., the amount in the plan or account and the primary and secondary beneficiaries.

❏ Review your beneficiaries and make changes as necessary.

❏ Review your overall plan for retirement and makes changes as necessary.

❏ Begin planning NOW if you do not have a retirement plan.

❏ Call 1-800-937-2700 and request Form SA 7004.

❏ Review the Request for Earnings and Benefit Estimate Statement for accuracy. Make corrections as necessary.

# PENSION AND RETIREMENT INVENTORY _____ (Date)

| Plan\Account | Amount | Beneficiaries | |
|---|---|---|---|
| | | Primary | Secondary |
| | | | |
| | | | |
| | | | |
| | | | |
| | | | |
| | | | |
| | | | |

# CHAPTER 5

❑ Have you planned for the management of your assets and the payment of your bills if you become disabled or incompetent?

❑ Have you planned for a trusted individual to make medical decisions for you if you are unable to make them yourself?

❑ Have you planned for the distribution of your assets at your death?

❑ Have you appointed a guardian for your minor children?

❑ Does your estate plan meet your objectives?

❑ Make changes in your estate plan if it does not meet your objectives. Consult your attorney.

❑ Develop and implement an estate plan if you do not already have one. Consult an experienced estate planning attorney.

❑ Store the original documents in a safe place.

# CHAPTER 6

❑ Prepare an inventory of your credit cards.

❑ Request credit reports from Experian, Trans Union Corporation and Equifax.

❑ Review the reports from accuracy.

❑ Correct any mistakes.

❑ Prepare an inventory of the contents of your wallet.

## CREDIT CARD-INVENTORY____

| Company | Account Number | Phone No | Interest Rate | Fee |
|---------|----------------|----------|---------------|-----|
|         |                |          |               |     |
|         |                |          |               |     |
|         |                |          |               |     |
|         |                |          |               |     |
|         |                |          |               |     |
|         |                |          |               |     |

# CONTENTS OF WALLET (DATE)

---

---

---

---

---

---

---

---

# CHAPTER 7

**TAXES**

1. Locate tax returns from prior years and insert them in folders.

2. Collect and organize information about the year's income.

Sources of income:
- Wage and salary ( W-2).
- Interest income (1099-INT).
- Dividend income (1099-DIV).
- Seller-financed mortgage interest income.
- Business income (and expenses).
- Sales of stocks, securities and installment sales (1099-A) (1099-B) (1099-S).
- Sale, exchange or purchase of real estate.
- Sales of personal residence (include fixing-up expenses, expenses associated with selling your home and moving expenses).
- Rental income (and expenses).
- Royalty income.
- Income from pensions and annuities (1099-R).
- Partnerships, S Corporations, estates and trusts (K-1 schedules).
- Farm income (and expenses).

- Unemployment compensation.
- Social Security benefits.
- Railroad retirement benefits.
- IRA distributions.
- Alimony.
- IRA, Keogh, SEP, and SIMPLE contributions.

3. Collect and organize information about the year's deductions.

For example:
- Medical and dental expenses.
- Taxes (real estate and personal property).
- Mortgage interest.
- Home equity interest.
- Investment interest.
- Alimony paid.
- Charitable contributions.
- Child and dependent care expenses.
- Union and professional dues.
- Tax preparation fee.
- Safe deposit box.
- Unreimbursed employee business expenses.
- Certain legal and accounting fees.
- Casualty and theft losses.

# CHAPTER 9

## LOCATION OF IMPORTANT DOCUMENTS

**Item**                                                    **Location**

Will_____

Trust _____

Power of attorney _____

Medical power of attorney_____

Living will _____


Asset\debt information (Attach Inventory)

Property deeds _____

Other real estate documents _____

Savings bonds _____

Certificates of deposit, T-Bills _____

Stock certificates _____

Promissory notes_____

Limited partnerships _____


Insurance policies (Attach Inventory)

Home Inventory _____

Vacation Home Inventory _____

Pension, IRA, Keogh, 401(k) records

(Attach Inventory) _____

Employee benefit documents _____

Automobile _____

Other vehicle\boats title\registrations _____

Birth certificates _____

Death certificates _____

Marriage license _____

Military discharge papers _____

Passport_____

Tax returns _____

Credit Card Inventory (Attach Inventory) _____

Any other legal documents _____

# BANKS AND CREDIT UNIONS

Bank and Address

_____

_____

_____

_____

_____

## SAFE DEPOSIT BOX

| Bank and Address | Number | Who Has Access | Location of Key |
|---|---|---|---|
| _____ | _____ | _____ | _____ |
| _____ | _____ | _____ | _____ |
| _____ | _____ | _____ | _____ |
| _____ | _____ | _____ | _____ |
| _____ | _____ | _____ | _____ |

# MEDICAL INFORMATION

Doctors

| Name | Phone | Address |
|------|-------|---------|
| _____ | _____ | _____ |
| _____ | _____ | _____ |
| _____ | _____ | _____ |
| _____ | _____ | _____ |

Other Health Personnel

| Name and Title | Phone | Address |
|----------------|-------|---------|
| _____ | _____ | _____ |
| _____ | _____ | _____ |
| _____ | _____ | _____ |

Current Medications

| Medication | Dose | Pharmacy |
|------------|------|----------|
| _____ | _____ | _____ |
| _____ | _____ | _____ |
| _____ | _____ | _____ |
| _____ | _____ | _____ |

## CONTACT IN AN EMERGENCY

| Name | Relationship | Phone | Address | | | | | | |
|------|--------------|-------|---------|--|--|--|--|--|--|
| | | | | | | | | | |
| | | | | | | | | | |
| | | | | | | | | | |
| | | | | | | | | | |
| | | | | | | | | | |
| | | | | | | | | | |
| | | | | | | | | | |
| | | | | | | | | | |

# FAMILY ADVISORS

Financial Advisor
Stock Broker
Name, Firm, Phone　　　　　　Address

_____　　_____

_____　　_____

_____　　_____

Accountant
Name, Firm, Phone　　　　　　Address

_____　　_____

_____　　_____

Attorney
Name, Firm, Phone　　　　　　Address

_____　　_____

_____　　_____

Insurance Agent
Name, Firm, Phone　　　　　　Address

_____　　_____

_____　　_____

# FUNERAL ARRANGEMENTS

Name of Funeral Home _____

Address _____

Phone _____

Location of Contract _____

Date of Contract _____

Arrangements _____

*Little Fugue in D Minor (Bach)*

_____

_____

# BURIAL ARRANGEMENTS

Name of Cemetery or place of Burial _____

Address _____

Phone _____

Location of Contract _____

Date of Contract _____

Arrangements _____

_____

_____

_____

# INDEX